The New Earth Is Born

Marika McGoldrick

The New Earth Is Born © 2022 Marika
McGoldrick

All rights reserved.

No part of this publication may be
reproduced, stored in a retrieval system, or
transmitted, in any form or by any means,
electronic, mechanical, photocopying,
recording or otherwise, without the prior
written permission of the presenters.

Marika McGoldrick asserts the moral right
to be identified as author of this work.

Presentation by *BookLeaf Publishing*

Web: www.bookleafpub.com

E-mail: info@bookleafpub.com

ISBN: 978-93-95255-29-5

First edition 2022

The World Is Like A Big Garden

The world is like a big garden,
If you want to feel peace, embody peace.
If you want to experience love, embody love.
If you want to sense kindness, embody kindness.

The transformation starts by yourself, through
your true self.

It will unconsciously plant the same seeds in
your neighbour, through this beautiful door, the
door of mirroring, by observing.

These wonderful seeds will grow, until they
naturally flow, in the entire humanity, with
humility, in order to connect with Mother Earth
and with respect.

The world is like a big garden, waiting to be
transformed...
Transformed into heaven.

Healthy Relationships

What do healthy relationships mean?
A mutual understanding of each other's values,
needs, boundaries, expectations.
A mutual desire of growing together.
A mutual willingness to support and challenge
each other.
A mutual respect for each other's truth.
A mutual agreement to communicate effectively.

Being able to take space and make space,
Being able to give and receive.

It is like an endless dance,
Speaking or responding,
Leading or following,
Loving or being loved.

Visualisation

An image, a picture, stuck in our minds.
Details, colours, shapes, emotions.
As soon as we visualise this clear picture,
Our own state can change.
We can feel happy, playful, anxious, depressed.
Any type of feelings.
These feelings will impact our bodies.
Whether with pain, or strength, or fear, or peace.
So many different states.

According to how we feel in our minds, in our
bodies,
Our natural reaction can lead us to be passive
and suffer from what comes next.

We can also decide to control this suffering, to
change it.
But first, we need to acknowledge it, to welcome
it.
Then we can decide to change the picture,
Exactly the way we want it to be.
This is called visualisation.

Visualisation is powerful.
Visualisation can help us heal, transform, take
ownership, take responsibility for our own life.

This is creation, empowerment, freedom from
the ego.
This is the potential of our minds.

Nature

5

Nature is our birthright.
Nature nurtures our hearts.
Nature supports our footsteps.
Nature holds our physical bodies.
Nature replenishes our souls.
Nature heals our minds.

Flowers,
Trees,
Oceans,
Rivers,
Beaches,
Mountains.

They make us feel part of a bigger picture, a
bigger purpose.
The vibrant colours, the cycle of life.

Nature lives within us,
And we live within nature.

Temple

What is a temple?
A sacred space to honour, to give, to receive,
A sacred space to be of service...
And the first person we serve...
Is us!
To create a temple within us,
We need to centre, to align, to love,
Our minds, our bodies, our spirits.

Sacred Animals

I had few dreams about animals,
Powerful dreams.
Dreams about dolphins, about whales, about
elephants.

I sensed the sacredness of these majestic
creatures.

They are much more sensitive, intelligent,
intuitive, as we could possibly imagine!
They are full of wisdom and we have so much to
learn from them.

They teach us strength, stability, and also peace,
playfulness, power, without forgetting
cooperation, communication, confidence.

They are keepers of the land, keepers of the
ocean, keepers of history.

They are sacred animals.

Transitions

Sometimes we catch ourselves between two
worlds,
Sometimes we struggle between two states,
Sometimes we just resist what is coming our
way.

Change, unknown, uncertainty can sometimes
reveal our doubts, our fears, our questions.

Transitions are part of life,
And if we become aware of them,
We become more enlightened.

The more we resist the new,
The more we hurt ourselves.
Transitions teach us patience, growth, faith,
trust.
Transitions are the opportunity to step out of the
comfort zone,
And experience a mystic energy.

The more we experience, the more we grow.
Nature is full of transitions.
The day and the night,
The four seasons,
The new moon and the full moon,

The caterpillar and the butterfly.

When we embrace transitions,
We allow ourselves to flow and be in sync with
the present energy by surrendering.
Being present brings awareness,
And awareness brings freedom.

I thank

I thank this abundant life that I have co-created
with this invisible strength.
I thank this Earth that I play on.
I thank this sky for inspiring me when I look up.
I thank the air, the earth, the water, the fire, for
being a part of me and the world around us.
I thank this body for carrying me.
I thank this breath, this life force, this chi, this
power within me.
Without this breath, what would I be?

The Bridge

I am here, in front of you.
You are looking at me,
Your eyes full of heaviness.

You are expecting me to move, to talk.
But instead,
I deeply look into your eyes.
I deeply look into your eyes,
And I feel what you feel.

I see you,
Truly as you are.
I see what you feel.
I see what you need to express.

I am here, with you,
On this bridge that we both build together, to
meet.

We share this beautiful moment with no words,
Just you, and I,
Your essence and mine,
In this perfect silence,
Reflecting your own perfection,
And mine.

We Crave

12

As a human species, we crave to be with one
another.
We crave to be acknowledged,
We crave to be recognised,
We crave to belong,
We crave to be understood.

We crave these so much that we can lose our
communication.

We can become agitated,
We can become frustrated,
We can become angry,
We can become sad.

What if we keep our hearts open as we share a
piece of ourselves with others?
What if our words, our behaviours could invite
others to hear us? To see us?

What if loving ourselves and others were the
answer, as we overall crave to be loved?

Harmony

13

Playing and laughing,
Listening and learning,
Growing and flowing,
Imagination and self-expression,
Caring and sharing,
Understanding and respecting,
Tolerance and balance,
Wildness and mindfulness,
Consciousness and gratefulness,
Dreaming and believing,
Collaborating and empowering,
Enlightening and loving,
They are all key,
To live in harmony,
With the Earth and humanity,
Feeling happy and free.

Memories

Memories can be powerful.
Memories can get stored in our brains, in our
bodies, in our hearts.

When we share our stories,
We share a piece of ourselves,
We share a piece of our souls,
Of what has been planted in it.

Memories can be passed on from generation to
generation.
Until memories become tales.
Then a tale allows us to grow by taking
whatever we need or want from it.
A tale allows us to learn from the past to create a
better future.

A tale, a story, a memory,
A piece of our souls which transmits the wisdom
of our time.

Mastery Of My Life

In a world which is driven by profitability, and
money, I observe.
I observe how much I love taking my time to
think,
Taking my time to understand,
Taking my time to interact with another being,
Taking my time to walk,

Taking my time to laugh,
Taking my time before speaking or answering,
enjoying these beautiful silences,
Taking my time to be kind,
Taking my time to love,
Taking my time to look after myself,
Taking my time to enjoy and explore the world
around me.

In a world which is driven by profitability, and
money,
Taking my time is seen as being slow, too slow,
in a very fast-paced environment.
But still, I take my time.

Time allows me to pour my heart, in every
single thing I do, with the intention of love.

Devotion for intention.
A life of quality instead of quantity.
I take my time to love, to be, this is the mastery
of my life.

To All The Lightworkers

To all the lightworkers,
Whether you do healing, or channelling, or
spiritual music, or art, or psychic readings, or
writing, or meditating, or helping the
environment.

You are here to elevate people to a higher level
of consciousness.
You are here to bring change.
You are here to remove fear.
You are here to light up the undiscovered.

It requires you to speak up your truth.
It requires you to stand up for equality.
It requires self-empowerment.

It is a lot of effort, a lot of energy,
A lot of inner knowledge, a lot of courage, a lot
of determination.

To all the lightworkers,
You are doing so well!
You are on the right path!
You make the world a better place!

Remember to trust your intuition.
Remember to be kind to yourself.
Remember to love yourself.
Remember that the universe won't judge you as
you are already doing so much!

You deserve as much love and compassion as
you give to others.

Remember that you are unique,
This uniqueness is precious and is your strength.
Remember that you have a big family of soul
lightworkers with you, supporting you.
Remember that we are unity, we are love, we are
one.

Our Difference Is Our Strength

19

The world is full of different cultures, religions, traditions.
Where some see threats,
Others see opportunities.
Opportunities to connect and learn from each other.
Connecting can lead to respect.
Respect can lead to understanding.
Understanding can lead to compassion.
And compassion can lead to love.

Love

When was the last time you touched someone?
Gave a hug to someone?
Said a nice word to someone?
Did a favour to someone?
How often do you do it?

Now think about yourself.
And ask the same questions to yourself.
When was the last time you touched yourself?
Gave a hug to yourself?
Said a nice word to yourself?
Did something which served you?
Helped, encouraged yourself?
How often do you do it?

And now compare your answers.
The world is full of beauty, of helpers, of
healers, of lovers.

Love is a precious energy,
So remember to spread it equally,
With balance and harmony.

Natural Beauty

Humanity is awakening and transforming,
Opening its eyes to this big reality,
Made of harmony and authenticity.

Air, earth, fire, water have a spirit,
Which needs to be respected and protected.

If we listen carefully,
To the mountain, the river and the tree,
We can feel the vibration and energy,
Coming from this natural beauty.

Their souls are abundantly powerful,
That's why with mindfulness,
We can hear their guidance,
Through love, faith, and patience.

What My Open Heart Does

22

When my heart is open,
I am vulnerable.
I get out of my comfort zone.
I make myself available to receive.
I make myself available to give.

When my heart is open,
I can connect deeply with myself.
I can connect deeply with others.

When my heart is open,
I walk in the world radiating kindness.
I walk in the world radiating love.

Silence

What is silence?
A complete absence of sound,
A pause, an in-between,
An invitation for a breath, for a contemplation of
the world.

Depending on how we deal with silence,
It gives information about ourselves, about
others.

For some of us, it brings impatience, anxiety,
frustration.
For some others, it brings peace, relaxation,
appreciation.

When we embrace silence,
We allow ourselves to be.

Silence is authentic,
Silence is real,
Silence is a feeling,
Silence is a situation,
Silence is pure,
Silence is beauty,
Silence is harmony,
Silence is the duality of sound,

Silence is vital.

Silence is what we need to hear our true selves.

Silence reflects what others' souls are
expressing.

When we are with another spirit,
Being able to hold silence and enjoy it,
Shows the level of connection between those
two beings.

Silence is key,
Silence is necessary,
Silence is freedom.

We Rise

Brothers, sisters, humans,
This is what we all are.
We all are in this earthy experience,
In this soulful adventure,
On this learning journey.

We all laugh,
We all cry,
We all feel,
We all experiment.

We all have joys,
We all have dreams,
We all have fears,
We all have memories.

As an individual, we get lost in the collective,
And through the collective, we find ourselves by
embracing our uniqueness.

And through this process,
Together we heal,
Together we rise.

The New Earth

While drinking this ancestral medicine, I had a vision.
And through movement, it became clearer.

Bringing this ancient wisdom into this modern era.
Mixing the best of the old and the new world.
Being able to let go of the past, while birthing the future.
Bringing back the tribal rites to life.
Sitting in circles, creating community.
Practicing active listening and sharing.
Making meaningful connections where we acknowledge each other with all our hearts and all our beings.
Where the truth is told.
Where our deepest shadows are revealed and healed.
Supporting one another, connected to the spirits.

While drinking this ancestral medicine, I had a vision.
And now I can see and feel how the New Earth is born.